MICHELLE OBAMA

MICHELLE OBAMA

FIRST LADY & ROLE MODEL

by Valerie Bodden

Content Consultant:
Carl Sferrazza Anthony
National First Ladies Library Historian

ABDO
Publishing Company

CREDITS

Published by ABDO Publishing Company, 8000 West 78th Street,
Edina, Minnesota 55439. Copyright © 2010 by Abdo Consulting
Group, Inc. International copyrights reserved in all countries. No
part of this book may be reproduced in any form without written
permission from the publisher. The Essential Library™ is a
trademark and logo of ABDO Publishing Company.

Printed in the United States.

 PRINTED ON RECYCLED PAPER

Editor: Melissa Johnson
Copy Editor: Paula Lewis
Interior Design and Production: Emily Love
Cover Design: Rebecca Daum

Library of Congress Cataloging-in-Publication Data
Bodden, Valerie.
  Michelle Obama : first lady & role model / by Valerie Bodden.
      p. cm. — (Essential lives)
  Includes bibliographical references and index.
  ISBN 978-1-60453-703-1
  1. Obama, Michelle, 1964- —Juvenile literature. 2. Presidents'
spouses—United States—Biography—Juvenile literature.
3. Legislators' spouses—United States—Biography—Juvenile
literature. 4. African American women lawyers—Illinois—
Chicago—Biography—Juvenile literature. 5. Chicago (Ill.)—
Biography—Juvenile literature I. Title.

  E909.O24B63 2010
  973.932092—dc22
  [B]
                                      2009009985

TABLE OF CONTENTS

Michelle Obama spoke at the 2008 Democratic National Convention.

MICHELLE OBAMA SPEAKS

It was August 25, 2008, the opening night of the Democratic National Convention. The voice of Craig Robinson rang out across the Pepsi Center in Denver, Colorado, as the crowd of 20,000 people broke into wild cheers. "Please join me in welcoming an impassioned public servant, a loving daughter, wife, and mother, my little sister, and our nation's next First Lady, Michelle Obama."[1] The crowd had been waiting for this moment. Michelle Obama, wife of Senator Barack Obama—soon to be the Democratic Party's nominee for president—was about to speak. As Michelle appeared onstage with a hug for her brother and smiles and waves for the audience, the cheers grew to a crescendo. Tall blue signs lettered simply "Michelle" bobbed among the crowd.

With the cameras rolling to carry her message to more than 20 million television viewers, Michelle began to speak. Rather than focusing on policies or issues, Michelle's speech introduced herself and her husband to the world. She emphasized that the two of them were not so different from any of the viewers. Michelle

Women Speakers

Before Michelle Obama, there was already a long tradition of candidates' spouses speaking at conventions. The first political spouse to address a convention was Eleanor Roosevelt. She spoke on behalf of her husband, incumbent President Franklin Roosevelt, in 1940. Other notable candidates' wives who have spoken at conventions include:

• Pat Nixon, 1972, wife of incumbent President Richard Nixon
• Nancy Reagan, 1984, wife of incumbent President Ronald Reagan
• Hillary Clinton, 1996, wife of incumbent President Bill Clinton
• Laura Bush, 2000, wife of Republican nominee (and later president) George W. Bush
• Teresa Heinz Kerry, 2004, wife of Democratic nominee John Kerry

said that she came to the convention as a sister, a wife, a mom, and a daughter. She said that her children were the most important thing to her and that their future was the reason she was involved in the election. She talked about her roots in Chicago's South Side, where her working-class parents had raised her and her brother. And she told about meeting Barack. She discovered that "even though he had this funny name, even though he'd grown up all the way across the continent in Hawaii," his family was a lot like hers.[2] They shared many of the same values: hard work, honesty, and respect for others.

The 2008 presidential primary had featured a woman and an African-American man competing for the Democratic nomination for the first time in history. Michelle talked about the women's rights and civil rights movements, saying, "I stand here today at the crosscurrents of that history, knowing that my piece of the American dream is a blessing hard won by those who came before me." She talked about change and about fighting "for the world as it should be."[3]

Concluding her speech on a personal note, Michelle talked about the presidential nominee as a husband and a father:

And in the end, after all that's happened these past 19 months, the Barack Obama I know today is the same man I fell in love with 19 years ago. He's the same man who drove me and our new baby daughter home from the hospital 10 years ago this summer, inching along at a snail's pace, peering anxiously at us in the rearview mirror, feeling the whole weight of her future in his hands, determined to give her everything he'd struggled so hard for himself.[4]

As she called for the country to make Barack Obama president of the United States, the crowd once again broke into cheers.

Talking about Race

Barack Obama was the first African American to ever be nominated by a major political party in the race for president. While Barack largely avoided talk about race on the campaign trail, his wife openly discussed racial issues. When some African-American voters questioned whether her husband was "black enough" to represent the African-American community, Michelle told them they were being ridiculous.

She did not hesitate to say that the effects of racism can still be felt in U.S. society. At a campaign stop in South Carolina in 2007, Michelle addressed a largely black audience. She spoke of their doubts that the country was ready to elect an African-American president. She said that such doubts sprang from the

veil of impossibility that keeps us down and keeps our children down—keeps us waiting and hoping for a turn that may never come. It's the bitter legacy of racism and discrimination and oppression in this country.[5]

By the end of the campaign, Michelle said the election had changed Americans' view of race. She believed it had opened the way for new conversations about the subject.

Michelle and Barack lead the parade to the presidential inauguration.

Many people rose from their seats, and some wiped
tears from their eyes.

First Lady

On November 4, 2008, voters answered
Michelle's call, electing Barack Obama the forty-
fourth president of the United States. Michelle later
described her feelings on that night:

I was proud as a wife, amazed as a citizen. I felt a sense of relief, a sense of calm, that the country I lived in was the country I thought I lived in.[6]

Two and a half months later, on January 20, 2009, Michelle and her husband stood on the West Front of the U.S. Capitol building in Washington DC for Barack's inauguration. A crowd of more than 1 million people stretched nearly two miles (3.2 km) across the National Mall to the Lincoln Memorial. The rooftops of nearby buildings were covered with onlookers. Others lined Pennsylvania Avenue waiting for the parade that would follow the ceremony.

With their daughters at her side, Michelle stood next to Barack. She held the Bible that Abraham Lincoln had used for his first presidential inauguration. She looked on, smiling slightly, as her husband placed his left hand on the Bible and took the oath of office. Barack Obama became

Style Icon

During Barack's 2008 presidential campaign, Michelle became known as a fashion icon. Much of the buzz about her on inauguration day centered on her clothing choices. For the swearing-in ceremony, Michelle wore a yellow-gold sheath dress and coat designed by Cuban-American designer Isabel Toledo. Later that night, she and her husband celebrated at ten inaugural balls. She wore a one-shouldered white gown by Taiwanese-born designer Jason Wu. Her dress choices won high marks from many fashion critics. Her sense of style landed her on the cover of the March 2009 issue of *Vogue*.

the nation's first African-American president—making Michelle its first African-American First Lady. Afterward, the couple shared a brief embrace. Then they turned and waved to the cheering crowd before Michelle sat to listen to her husband's inaugural address.

After the inauguration, Michelle, Barack, and their daughters led the inaugural parade in their limousine. Michelle and Barack got out to walk and to wave to their admirers. Many people had stood in the cold for hours in order to get a glimpse of the new president and his wife. After watching the rest of the two-hour inaugural parade, the Obamas finally entered the White House— their new home.

Becoming a Political Spouse

When Michelle married Barack Obama in 1992, she had no idea the road she was embarking on might

Kids' Inaugural Concert

The night before Barack's inauguration, Michelle cohosted the Kids' Inaugural Concert with Jill Biden, wife of the incoming vice president, Joe Biden. The event was held in honor of military families. Of the 14,000 children and parents in attendance, 4,000 were children of service members who had been invited to the concert free of charge. The crowd was treated to a performance by, among others, teen pop-rock band the Jonas Brothers. The Jonas Brothers also visited the White House the next evening to entertain the Obamas' daughters Malia and Sasha in a surprise visit arranged by Michelle.

one day lead her to the White House. Barack was not involved in politics at the time. When he wanted to enter the political world a few years after their marriage, Michelle confessed that she was "very wary of politics." She explained,

> When you are involved in politics, your life is an open book, and people can come in who don't necessarily have good intent. I'm pretty private, and like to surround myself with people that I trust and love. In politics you've got to open yourself to a lot of different people.[7]

Despite her reservations, Michelle gave her husband the go-ahead. He ran for the Illinois state senate, followed by the U.S. Senate, and then the presidency. At each step, she questioned the disruption politics would bring to their family and wondered whether the sacrifice would be worth it. Ultimately, she decided it would:

Running for Office?

Because of the strength of Michelle's speeches at the Democratic National Convention and on the campaign trail, some people have suggested she would make a good senator or president herself. In his book *The Audacity of Hope*, Barack wrote that if his wife ever ran against him for public office, he would certainly lose. Fortunately for him, Michelle has made it clear she has no interest in running for office.

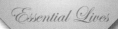

When we made the decision to get in this [presidential] race, there was a side of me that said, "Oh, no. This is going to be so personally disruptive—why put yourself through that?" But then I let myself dream about what his presidency would mean [to the nation and the world] and I get goose bumps.[8]

Michelle Obama became the first African-American First Lady in January 2009.

Michelle grew up on Chicago's South Side.

SOUTH SIDE GIRL

During her husband's presidential campaign, Michelle often spoke with pride of her roots on the South Side of Chicago. Born on January 17, 1964, Michelle LaVaughn Robinson was the second child of Fraser and

Marian Robinson. Her brother, Craig, had been born 16 months earlier.

Although they lived in Chicago, Michelle's family had roots in South Carolina, where her great-great-grandfather was a slave until the time of the Civil War. His son, Michelle's great-grandfather, Fraser Robinson Sr., lived with a white family during his teenage years. The family showed him the importance of education, and he later taught himself to read. Despite the fact that he had lost an arm as a boy, he became a prosperous shoemaker and newspaper salesman. Fraser Sr. emphasized the importance of education to his children, including Michelle's grandfather, Fraser Jr.

Although he was an excellent student, the only work Fraser Jr. could find was at a sawmill in South Carolina. Deciding that his chances would be better in the North, Fraser Jr. moved to Chicago. He was one of millions of African

South Carolina Roots

Little is known about Jim Robinson, Michelle's great-great-grandfather. It is believed that he was born around 1850. He was a slave on a rice plantation called Friendfield, near Georgetown, South Carolina, until the Civil War. Today, five of the slave cabins at Friendfield still stand. The small, white, wooden structures had no heat, no glass windows, and no plumbing.

Fraser Jr. and LaVaughn, Michelle's grandparents, moved back to Georgetown after they retired. Michelle often visited them there and frequently passed by the Friendfield gate. However, her grandfather never talked about her family's history at Friendfield. Michelle did not learn about it until she visited South Carolina during her husband's presidential campaign.

Americans who migrated from the South to cities in the North during the early and mid-twentieth century. This movement later became known as the Great Migration. The North did not offer as many opportunities as Fraser Jr. had hoped. He had a difficult time finding work and eventually took a job as a postal clerk.

WORKING-CLASS FAMILY

Michelle's father, Fraser III, was born in Chicago and spent most of his adult life working for the city. At the time Michelle was born, Fraser had just taken a job as a janitor with Chicago's water department. Over the years, he was promoted several times, eventually becoming an operating engineer with the department. Michelle's mother, Marian, stayed home to raise her two children. Although Fraser's salary was not large, he was able to provide for his family. Looking back on her youth, Michelle said, "The only amazing thing about my life is that a man like my father could raise a family of four on a single city worker's salary."[1]

One year after Michelle was born, her father was diagnosed with multiple sclerosis. Multiple sclerosis causes muscle tremors and weakness and gets worse over time. He continued to get up each day to go to work, even when he later needed to use a cane and then crutches to get around. He never complained about his situation. He simply got up early to make sure he had enough time to complete the painstaking task of getting ready for work. Even buttoning his shirt became a chore. Seeing her father struggle was part of the vital lesson Michelle's parents taught her: nothing in this world cannot be overcome if one puts his or her mind to it.

Chicago's South Side

During Chicago's early history, its South Side was settled by American-born whites. The first settlers were later joined by immigrants from Ireland, Poland, Lithuania, Germany, and Eastern Europe. During the early twentieth century, more than 500,000 African Americans left the southern United States to settle in Chicago. Many of them came to work in the city's steel mills, stockyards, and rail yards, which were located on the South Side. As African Americans began to settle there, whites moved out, creating a city that remained largely segregated until the 1960s.

Eventually, the South Side expanded until it bordered with an African-American community on Chicago's western edge. This became one of the country's largest African-American communities. Today, the South Side covers 60 percent of Chicago. It is made up of several neighborhoods, including South Shore and Hyde Park. Many of the neighborhoods are settled by middle-class families, although much of Chicago's poverty can also be found on the South Side. The Chicago White Sox and the University of Chicago are located in this part of the city. Many U.S. artists have found their inspiration on the South Side, including authors Richard Wright and Upton Sinclair, poet Gwendolyn Brooks, painter Archibald Motley Jr., sculptor Henry Moore, and musician Mahalia Jackson.

Marian Robinson, Michelle's mother, encouraged her children's education.

In addition to his work duties, Fraser volunteered as precinct captain for the Democratic Party in Chicago. He would often take Michelle with him as he traveled from door to door to register voters.

LIVING ON THE SOUTH SIDE

During Michelle's earliest years, the family lived in an African-American, working-class neighborhood on the South Side. A few years later, they moved to the traditionally white South Side community of South Shore, on the southern end of Lake Michigan. As more African-American families moved into the neighborhood, white families moved out, a process sometimes called white flight. Soon, the community was almost entirely African American. South Shore was a safe neighborhood. Kids could leave their bikes outside overnight without worrying that the bikes would be gone in the morning.

The Robinsons' new home was on the upper floor of a brick bungalow owned by Michelle's aunt. It had only one bedroom, so Michelle's parents divided the living room with a partition to create a small bedroom for Michelle and Craig to share.

The Robinson home was a hub of family activity. Relatives were constantly in and out of the house. On Saturdays, Michelle, Craig, and their parents spent the evening playing board games. The family had rules, too. Michelle and her brother could watch television for only one hour a day. They were expected to spend much of their free time reading or pursuing other interests. Michelle chose to play the piano, practicing so much that her mother would often have to tell her to stop. The children also had

Facing Discrimination

When the Robinson family moved to the mostly white neighborhood of South Shore, it was hard not to notice that white families soon moved out. Fraser and Marian were open with their children about such discrimination. They encouraged Michelle and Craig not to let it affect their lives. According to Craig, their parents would tell them, "Life's not fair. It's not. And you don't always get what you deserve, but you have to work hard to get what you want. And then sometimes you don't get it; even if you work hard and do all the right things, you don't get it."[3] Fraser also told his children that one day a black person would be president.

chores such as washing dishes and cleaning the bathroom. Although their father rarely yelled, both kids hated to disappoint him. Craig said,

> We always felt like we couldn't let Dad down because he worked so hard for us. My sister and I, if one of us ever got in trouble with my father, we'd both be crying. We'd both be like, "Oh, my God, Dad's upset. How could we do this to him?"[2]

A Bright Student

Fraser and Marian Robinson valued education and taught both Craig and Michelle to read before they entered school. The children attended Bryn Mawr Elementary School (now called Bouchet Math and Science Academy), where both skipped second grade. In sixth grade, Michelle was enrolled in her school's gifted program. This gave her the opportunity to study French and take a biology course at nearby Kennedy-King Community College. Michelle's parents encouraged their children to focus on their education and emphasized the importance of asking questions. Marian later said,

> *More important, even, than learning to read and write was to teach them to think. We told them, "Make sure you respect your teachers, but don't hesitate to question them. Don't even allow us to just say anything to you. Ask us why."*[4]

After graduating second in her eighth grade class, Michelle attended the Whitney M. Young Magnet High School. This new public high school brought together some of the brightest students from across Chicago. The school was located several miles from her home. It took Michelle half an hour or more to get to school. She had to travel by bus and elevated train and then walk from the train station to the school. Michelle chose to make this trip rather than attend the public school in her neighborhood, which was just down the street from her home. Several of Michelle's teachers said that the decision to attend Whitney M. Young was rather experimental at the time. "I think you had to be the sort of person and the sort of family that would put education above everything else," English teacher Dagny Bloland explained.[5]

Whitney M. Young School

The Whitney M. Young Magnet High School was founded in 1975. Its goal was to change Chicago's segregated public schools. As it did during Michelle's time as a student, the school today has a very diverse student body. Approximately 31 percent of the school's students are black, 30 percent are Caucasian, 21 percent are Hispanic, and 18 percent are Asian. The school is known for its high educational standards. Many of its students go on to attend prestigious colleges, such as Harvard, Yale, Stanford, and Duke.

Just as she had been in grade school, Michelle was a dedicated student throughout her high school years. She enrolled in several honors courses. Although she sometimes struggled with tests, she made the school's honor roll every year and became a member of the National Honor Society. She was elected treasurer of her senior class as well.

One activity Michelle was not involved in was sports. Michelle was five feet eleven inches tall and an excellent basketball player. She chose to stay off the basketball court, however, partly because she was intensely competitive and could not stand to lose. She also did not want people to compare her to Craig, who was a star basketball player. According to her brother, Michelle also chose not to compete because she did not want to do what everyone expected of her. "That's the best way to get her not to do something," he said. "She didn't want to play just because she was tall and black and athletic."[6]

Michelle's brother, Craig, grew up to become a college basketball coach.

Princeton University had a predominately white student body when Michelle was a student.

ON TO PRINCETON

While Michelle was still in high school, Craig began his first year at Princeton University. When it was her turn to choose a college, Michelle decided to follow him there. Some of Michelle's teachers told her not to apply to

Princeton. They said her test scores and grades were not high enough to get into the Ivy League school. Michelle decided, though, that if her brother could attend Princeton, she could too. She was right.

A New World

Michelle arrived at Princeton in the fall of 1981. She was one of only 94 black students in her freshman class of 1,100 people. Having grown up in a community where African Americans were in the majority, she felt out of her element in this new environment. To complicate matters, Michelle and the other black and Hispanic students in her class had been brought to campus a few weeks before the rest of the class. When the other students arrived, the school seemed to separate along racial lines. Michelle spent most of her time with other black students.

Although she had a number of good friends, Michelle often felt isolated. She became aware for

Head Coach

Craig Robinson was one of Princeton's all-time leading scorers in basketball. After graduation, he was drafted by the Philadelphia 76ers. He was cut, however, and went to play professional basketball in Europe. Upon returning to the United States, Craig obtained his Master of Business Administration and took a job with an investment company. Eventually, he realized that he was not passionate about what he was doing. At the age of 37, he quit his job to become a basketball coach. In April 2008, he became head coach at Oregon State University.

White Roommate

During her freshman year at Princeton, one of Michelle's roommates was a white woman named Catherine Donnelly. Although Michelle did not know it at the time, Catherine's mother demanded that her daughter be reassigned to a room with a white roommate. The request was denied. Catherine soon found that Michelle was a likeable woman, although the two never became close friends. "Here was a really smart black woman who I found charming, interesting, and funny," Catherine later said. "Just by virtue of having different color skin, we weren't going to be friends."[1] Before the end of the year, Catherine had moved into a larger dorm room. She and Michelle saw little more of each other.

the first time what it meant to be a minority. She noticed that many of the white students with whom she had classes would ignore her outside of class, pretending not to see her if their paths happened to cross. Other African–American students at Princeton, too, said that for the first time they had to confront what it meant to be black. Most felt like they did not fit in.

The social scene at Princeton centered on "eating clubs." Clubs selected their members, who ate and debated together in clubhouses. Although some black students worked at these clubs, few were members. Instead, many of them, including Michelle, spent much of their time at the Third World Center (now known as the Carl A. Fields Center for Equality and Understanding). The center was a gathering place for minority students on campus, who socialized and attended presentations there. Michelle joined the center's governing board and helped coordinate an after-school literacy program for children of the surrounding neighborhood.

WRITING ABOUT RACE

Despite her difficulties in adjusting to campus life, Michelle threw herself into her course work. She majored in sociology and minored in African-American studies. Determined to succeed, Michelle woke early every day in order to study. According to friends, both Michelle and Craig wanted to do well for the sake of their parents, who had not graduated from college.

·By the time she was a senior, Michelle was still wrestling with the issue of race and how it affected her experience at Princeton. She explored the issue further in her senior thesis, titled "Princeton-Educated Blacks and the Black

Princeton University

Originally known as the College of New Jersey, Princeton was founded in 1746. It is the fourth-oldest college in the nation. The 500-acre (202.3-ha) campus is located in Princeton, New Jersey. It is the site of Nassau Hall, where the U.S. government met for several months in 1783. In 2009, Princeton had 4,850 undergraduates and nearly 2,300 graduate students.

No Limits

Michelle never forgot what it was like to have people—such as the teachers who told her not to apply to Princeton—place limits on her. In a speech at Benedict College in 2008, Michelle told her mostly black audience, "We are confronted with the doubters. People who tell us what we can't do. You're not ready. You're not good enough. You're not smart enough. . . . [T]he truth is there are millions of shining little lights just like me all over this country. Kids living in the shadows, being told by their own communities what they can and cannot do. This is an opportunity for all of us to send a different message to all those shining lights."[4]

Community." In the thesis, she examined the experiences of black students at Princeton. She wrote that such an examination was important because "as more Blacks begin attending predominantly White universities it will be helpful to know how their experiences in these universities affect their future attitudes."[2]

Of her own time at Princeton, Michelle wrote:

My experiences at Princeton have made me far more aware of my "Blackness" than ever before. I have found that at Princeton no matter how liberal and open-minded some of my White professors and classmates try to be toward me, I sometimes feel like a visitor on campus; as if I really don't belong. Regardless of the circumstances under which I interact with Whites at Princeton, it often seems as if, to them, I will always be Black first and a student second.[3]

In order to gain the perspectives of other Princeton students, Michelle sent a survey to 400 black Princeton alumni. In it, she asked graduates how much time they spent with blacks and whites before, during, and after their time at Princeton. She asked with which group they felt more comfortable. She also asked how they felt about lower-class African Americans. And, she asked whether they believed that it was their duty to help improve conditions for African Americans less fortunate than themselves.

Michelle had hoped to find that even though black alumni

Senior Thesis

Michelle's senior thesis was shelved in Princeton's library and was available to the public. When Barack decided to run for president, his campaign staff asked that Princeton restrict access to the thesis until after the election. Princeton cooperated, but it raised the suspicions of some voters and journalists. They complained that Barack had always claimed to run a transparent campaign. In response, the campaign released the thesis to an online political newspaper, *Politico*, which posted the document on its Web site in February 2008.

Barack's opponents pointed to the thesis as evidence that Michelle was a militant racist in favor of racial separatism and maintaining separate social structures or cultures for blacks and whites. Supporters pointed out, however, that Michelle was trying to identify the prevailing attitudes of Princeton alumni. She posed the question for scientific research and did not suggest her own opinion on the answer. They also argued that a document she had written more than 20 years before the campaign was not relevant to her husband's presidential bid.

might begin to identify more with whites as they reached higher levels of education, they would still identify with the African-American community to some degree. Instead, the answers of the 100 or so alumni who responded to her survey indicated that as blacks became more educated and achieved financial success, they tended to move away from their identification with other blacks. She worried that she saw the same happening in her own life:

> ...[A]s I enter my final year at Princeton, I find myself striving for many of the same goals as my White classmates— acceptance to a prestigious graduate or professional school or a high paying position in a successful corporation. Thus, my goals after Princeton are not as clear as before.[5]

Yet, Michelle wrote that she hoped to one day use the education and opportunities she had been given to help the African-American community.

Michelle graduated from Princeton in 1985 with a degree in sociology.

Harvard University is located in Cambridge, Massachusetts.

STUDYING THE LAW

fter graduating from Princeton with honors in 1985, Michelle entered Harvard Law School. Earlier, a Princeton professor had encouraged her to reconsider. Unlike when she had applied to Princeton, her professor's concern was not over her grades. Instead, she worried that Michelle would not be happy with the path she had chosen. As in the past, Michelle did not heed her teachers.

When she arrived at Harvard in the fall of 1985, Michelle noticed some of the same racial issues that had marked her time at Princeton. By now, though, the 21-year-old was more comfortable with her "blackness," and she did not find the adjustment to Harvard as difficult as the transition to Princeton had been. According to her law school adviser, Charles J. Ogletree, Michelle had undergone a transformation between her time at Princeton and her arrival at Harvard:

> *Princeton was a real crossroads of identity for Michelle. The question [for her] was whether I retain my identity given by my African-American parents, or whether the education from an elite*

Harvard Law School

Located in Cambridge, Massachusetts, Harvard Law School is one of the most prestigious law schools in the country. Many of its alumni have achieved important positions. As of 2008, six of the nine justices on the U.S. Supreme Court were former Harvard Law students. In addition, seven graduates of Harvard have served as U.S. solicitors general, the lawyer who represents the United States before the Supreme Court, and 12 have been elected governor. Eight U.S. presidents have earned degrees in law or other fields from Harvard.

university has transformed me into something different than what they made me. By the time she got to Harvard she had answered the question. She could be both brilliant and black.[1]

Michelle and Barack at Harvard

Michelle graduated from Harvard Law School in the spring of 1988. In the fall of that year, Barack began his first semester at the school. Although their paths never crossed at Harvard, Michelle and Barack had some of the same professors. One of them, Professor Charles Ogletree, later joined Barack's presidential campaign team as a senior adviser. In January 2009, just after Barack was sworn in as the nation's forty-fourth president, Ogletree wrote about the new commander-in-chief and his wife during their time at Harvard.

In his reflection, Ogletree wrote that both Barack and Michelle had been exceptional students. Barack, he said, was a curious student who kept professors on their toes by asking questions about the fine points of the law. And Michelle struck him as a student dedicated to both her studies and her work with the Legal Aid Bureau. Ogletree had once thought that the future in politics might lie with her:

Based upon her intelligence, drive, warm personality, and deep conviction to spend her legal career in pursuit of public service, I imagined then that she would become the first African-American woman to serve in the United States Senate.[2]

GETTING INVOLVED

As she had in the past, Michelle proved to be an excellent student. Unlike her future husband, Barack Obama, who would enter Harvard the semester after she graduated, Michelle was not overly political or outspoken. According to Professor Randall Kennedy, "When [Barack] spoke, people got quiet and listened. Michelle had a more modest, quieter, lower profile."[3] Although she was quiet, Michelle's professors remembered her as a student who could form strong, compelling arguments to support her ideas.

Michelle also found ways to become involved on campus. She participated in demonstrations to demand that the school admit more minority students and hire more minority professors. She also worked with the school's administration to help attract minorities to campus.

Michelle joined the school's *BlackLetter Journal*, which had been founded in the early 1980s. It was an alternative to the *Harvard Law Review* and other law journals that were run by mostly white students. The *BlackLetter Journal* focused on how the law affected minorities.

Michelle also joined the Black Law Students Association. It was a

Affirmative Action

According to some accounts, Michelle was admitted to both Princeton and Harvard as a result of affirmative action programs. Affirmative action programs are intended to increase the number of minorities at schools. One of her friends from Harvard, Verna Williams, said that although black students at the law school sometimes felt as if they were seen as charity cases, Michelle was comfortable with the fact that she had benefitted from affirmative action. Michelle's aides in the Obama campaign, however, insisted that Michelle was not an affirmative action student but was instead admitted to Princeton as a "legacy" student because her brother attended the school. They said she earned acceptance to Harvard through her academic achievements at Princeton.

Barack entered Harvard Law School the autumn after Michelle graduated.

social club for black students, but it also served as a support network and helped students further their legal careers. To help students learn about the career choices available to them after law school, Michelle helped organize an association event in which black alumni working in government, public service, and private practice were brought together to talk about their respective fields. The symposium became an annual event.

SERVING THE POOR

Michelle spent much of her time at Harvard at Gannett House, the same building where her future husband would one day serve as the first African-American president of the *Harvard Law Review*. While Barack would work on the top floors of the building, however, Michelle passed her days on a lower floor, in the office of the Harvard Legal Aid Bureau. Unlike the other organizations to which she belonged, the bureau was multiracial. Although the students who made it up did not come from the same backgrounds, they shared a common ideology—a desire to serve—that helped them form friendships.

Through the bureau, Harvard law students helped local residents who were too poor to pay for a lawyer. The students ran the office, and each dedicated at least 20 hours a week to working there. They also spent

Harvard Legal Aid Bureau

Founded in 1913, the Harvard Legal Aid Bureau is the oldest organization of its kind in the country. As the student lawyers with the bureau provide free legal services to low-income residents, they also gain practical law experience. Many former legal aid members have gone on to use that experience in public service. Among notable alumni of the Harvard Legal Aid Bureau are:

• William Brennan Jr. (1931), former associate justice, U.S. Supreme Court

• Frank Coffin (1943), former federal judge, U.S. Court of Appeals, First Circuit

• Daniel O'Hern (1957), former justice, New Jersey Supreme Court

• Howard Learner (1980), executive director, Environmental Law & Policy Center

• Deval Patrick (1982), governor, Massachusetts

Yearbook Message

When Michelle finished Harvard Law School in 1988, her parents had the opportunity to purchase space in her yearbook. Most of the other parents who purchased space wrote sentimental messages of congratulation. But Michelle's parents chose to send a humorous message: "We knew you would do this fifteen years ago when we could never make you shut up."[5]

time in the courtroom representing clients with the guidance of a licensed attorney. Many of the cases taken on by the Legal Aid Bureau involved disputes between landlords and tenants, including evictions. Other cases involved clients who had problems with government benefits or who were involved in divorce or child custody cases.

Michelle's colleagues at the Legal Aid Bureau thought of her as a compassionate, dedicated lawyer. Ronald Torbert, president of the bureau, said of Michelle,

I remember being struck almost immediately by—although she smiled a lot and we had a lot of fun—[how she had] a serious side to her, the things she thought about. She was very mature, very very bright, she handled some of the more complex landlord-and-tenant issues. I just remember her being very serious about the work she did, and she really cared a lot about the people she worked with.[4]

Professor Charles Ogletree taught both Michelle and Barack at Harvard.

Michelle and Barack spent Christmas together in Hawaii in 1989.

BARACK'S MENTOR

After graduating from Harvard Law School in 1988, Michelle took a job with the corporate law firm Sidley & Austin in Chicago. She chose the firm in part because she had student loans to repay. The position offered a starting salary of $65,000, a relatively large amount at that time, especially for a young person's first professional job. The firm was in her hometown, which also influenced her decision. Michelle's parents had made it clear to her that part of the reason communities often suffered was that their young people left to get their educations and never returned. They said that if a few of those people came back, they could make a huge difference. Michelle returned to the neighborhood she had left, living with her parents and commuting to her office in the Chase Tower in downtown Chicago.

Corporate Lawyer

At Sidley, Michelle was part of the marketing group, which represented advertising agencies, car companies, and other organizations that had a product to sell. From the beginning, though, Michelle was dissatisfied

Barney the Dinosaur

As part of her work at Sidley & Austin, Michelle handled the trademark of Barney, the purple dinosaur character from the Public Broadcasting Service (PBS) show *Barney & Friends*. The show was new at the time, and Michelle's superiors felt that she was suited to the project because of her public interest background. Michelle's job was to ensure that Barney merchandise was protected by trademark. She also worked with stations that wanted to air the show. Although she had not done much of this type of work in the past, her colleagues said that Michelle did well on the project.

with her job. Other members of the marketing group believed that their division took on the most interesting projects in the firm. However, Michelle frequently asked her division's head, Quincy White, for more interesting and challenging projects. White did not believe that any project he gave her would have made her happy. "I couldn't give her something that would meet her sense of ambition to change the world," he later said.[1]

THE SUMMER ASSOCIATE

Only a year after she had started at Sidley & Austin, in the summer of 1989, Michelle was assigned to mentor summer associate Barack Obama, who had just finished his first year at Harvard Law School. Many of the lawyers in the firm were excited about Barack's arrival. They praised him as handsome, intelligent, and a standout at Harvard. Michelle,

High Standards

Michelle had a reputation with her family for having high standards when it came to boyfriends. When she brought Barack home to meet her family, her parents and brother figured Barack would not last long. In order to help her evaluate Barack's character, Michelle asked Craig to play a game of basketball with him. Although Barack had played basketball in high school, he was no match for Craig, who had played professionally in Europe. Still, he was willing to take the court. After their game, Craig reported to his sister that Barack was a team player and was self-confident but not a show-off.

however, was wary of meeting him. She later explained why:

> He sounded too good to be true. I had dated a lot of brothers who had this kind of reputation coming in, so I figured he was one of these smooth brothers who could talk straight and impress people.[2]

Despite her reservations, it was Michelle's job as his mentor to make Barack feel welcome at Sidley. She invited him to lunch his first day on the job. To her surprise, she discovered that she liked him, finding him bright and easy to talk to.

Barack Obama

Barack Obama was born on August 4, 1961, in Honolulu, Hawaii, two years after the islands became the fiftieth state. His father, Barack Obama Sr., had grown up in a Kenyan village, and his mother, Ann Dunham, was raised in a small town in Kansas. The two met at the University of Hawaii.

Barack's parents divorced when he was two years old. He saw his father only once after that. Barack was raised by his mother and grandparents in Honolulu. He also spent four years of his childhood in Indonesia with his mother and an Indonesian stepfather.

After graduating from Honolulu's Punahou School in 1979, Barack briefly attended Occidental College in Los Angeles. He transferred to Columbia University in New York City and graduated in 1983. He found work in New York City with Business International Corporation and the New York Public Interest Research Group. In 1985, he moved to Chicago to become a community organizer. In that role, he worked with people in communities suffering job losses due to the closing of steel plants. He helped them find ways to improve schools and deal with high crime and unemployment rates. In 1988, Barack left his work in Chicago to attend Harvard Law School and graduated in 1991.

Barack liked Michelle, too. He later said that during that first lunch, he noticed in Michelle

> *a glimmer that danced across her round, dark eyes whenever I looked at her, the slightest hint of uncertainty, as if, deep inside, she knew how fragile things really were, and that if she ever let go, even for a moment, all her plans might quickly unravel.[3]*

He decided that he wanted to get to know her better and asked her out. Michelle thought it would be strange for her to date the man she was mentoring and said no. Barack persisted, though, and he eventually convinced her. After a company picnic, he bought her ice cream, and the two soon became a couple.

As they learned more about one another, Michelle and Barack realized how very different they were. This only seemed to add to their attraction for one another.

Barack's Rock

Throughout his life, Barack has been surrounded by strong women—his mother, his grandmother, and Michelle. He credits these three women with providing his inspiration. After winning the 2008 presidential election, Barack acknowledged his debt to the woman who had once been his law firm mentor, saying, "I would not be standing here tonight without the unyielding support of my best friend for the last 16 years, the rock of our family and the love of my life, our nation's next First Lady, Michelle Obama."[4]

Barack was the son of a black father from Kenya and a white mother from the United States. He had spent his youth in Hawaii and Indonesia. With a past so far removed from hers, Barack seemed exotic to Michelle. For his part, Barack was enchanted by Michelle's close-knit family.

Wanting to Make a Difference

Around the time that Michelle and Barack started dating, he took her to a meeting in a church basement on Chicago's South Side. Before attending Harvard, Barack had served as a community organizer in this part of the city. He had decided to attend Harvard and earn his law degree so he could help people more effectively. He was returning to talk to a group he had worked with in the past. As he took off his suit coat and tie, Michelle watched him change from a lawyer into someone who could relate to

Community Relations

Michelle described her feelings when she went with Barack to the community meeting: "People found something real and authentic in what he was saying, and it resonated with me. And I knew then and there that Barack Obama was the real deal."[5]

Barack's commitment to public service would later lead him to a career in politics. Photo © Marc PoKempner

the single mothers and grandparents in this poor community. She was impressed. She was also touched by his message, as he encouraged his audience to work toward changing "the world as it is" into "the world as it should be."[6]

After Barack and Michelle had
spent the summer together, it was
time for Barack to return to Harvard.
The couple maintained a long-
distance relationship. Only a few
months later, Michelle's father died
unexpectedly after undergoing kidney
surgery. Michelle was devastated.
Afterward, she also had to deal with
the death of one of her best friends,
Suzanne Alele, who died of cancer
at the age of 25. Losing both her
father and her friend made Michelle
rethink what she was doing with her
own life:

> *I was confronted for the first time in*
> *my life with the fact that nothing was*
> *really guaranteed. One of the things I*
> *remembered about Suzanne is she always*
> *made decisions that would make her*
> *happy and create a level of fulfillment.*
> *She was less concerned with pleasing*
> *other people, and thank God. Was I*
> *waking up every morning feeling excited*

Michelle's Father

Michelle was extremely
close to her father. His
death impacted not only
her desire to find a more
meaningful career but
also her idea of what success meant. She began to
think of her achievements
in terms of making her
father proud. Michelle
continually asked herself
what her father would
think about what she was
doing, whether in her
career or her personal life.
During Barack's presiden-
tial campaign, Michelle
said that thinking of her
father was what kept her
grounded no matter how
famous she and her hus-
band became.

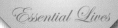

about work and the work I was doing? I needed to figure out what I really loved.[7]

Michelle was coming to understand that, as for Barack, the conventional path was not for her. She wanted to feel passionate about her job, and she wanted to help people. At this point, she was not sure what she really loved, but she knew it was not practicing corporate law.

*Michelle and Barack worked at Sidley & Austin,
located in the Chase Tower in downtown Chicago.*

Michelle has been dedicated to helping others throughout her life.
Photo © Marc PoKempner

PUBLIC SERVICE

lthough Michelle was not content at her job, she remained with Sidley & Austin until Barack graduated from Harvard Law School in 1991 and moved to Chicago. At that point, the firm offered him a full-time position, but he turned it down. Instead, he chose to take a position with a small civil rights law firm. He also taught at the University of Chicago Law School. Michelle, too, decided that she was ready to leave corporate law to work in the public service sector.

In her search for a new job, Michelle met with Valerie Jarrett, the deputy chief of staff for Mayor Richard M. Daley of Chicago. Jarrett was so impressed by Michelle that she offered her a job as an assistant to the mayor. Michelle did not accept the position right away. Instead, she asked Jarrett to meet with her and Barack to discuss the job further. She explained that Barack wanted to know who would be protecting her interests and making sure she flourished in the new position. After meeting with Jarrett, Barack was comfortable with the idea of Michelle taking the job, and she accepted.

Not Harsh, but Firm

Michelle's colleagues remembered her as someone who could get things done and who was honest with her employees. On one occasion, a staff member working for Michelle in the city government asked for a promotion. Michelle denied the request. She pointed out to the staff member all the reasons she was not qualified for it. According to another colleague, Michelle was not harsh in her criticism, but she was firm.

Michelle's new job as an assistant to the mayor involved a significant pay cut from what she had been earning at Sidley. The job in the mayor's office paid $60,000 a year—less than the starting salary she had received at Sidley as a graduate fresh from law school. Michelle was not too worried about the money, though. She was more concerned with finding satisfaction in her work.

Soon after Michelle had begun to work for the mayor, Valerie Jarrett was promoted to lead the city's department of planning and economic development. Jarrett brought Michelle with her to the new department. As assistant commissioner, Michelle worked to improve Chicago's economy.

BECOMING MRS. OBAMA

In 1991, Michelle was at a crossroads not only in her career but also in her relationship with Barack.

Valerie Jarrett

Similar to Michelle, Valerie Jarrett once worked in corporate law and left it to enter the public sector. After meeting with Michelle and Barack in 1991, she became one of the couple's most trusted friends. Jarrett was instrumental in helping Barack learn the ways of Chicago politics and later served on his presidential campaign. After being elected president, Barack named Jarrett a senior adviser in his administration.

She wanted to get married, but he did not. Michelle, who had grown up with two loving parents in her life, thought marriage was an important step in a relationship. Barack, whose parents had divorced early, was not sure that marriage was necessary. The issue caused frequent arguments.

The couple was again arguing over marriage one night at an upscale Chicago restaurant. Michelle told Barack that it was time for him to commit to their relationship, and he, as usual, disagreed. When the dessert came, though, Michelle found a box with an engagement ring in it on her plate. As she later recalled, "He said, 'That kind of shuts you up, doesn't it?' . . . I was so shocked and sort of a little embarrassed because he did sort of shut me up."[1]

Barack and Michelle were married on October 3, 1992, at Chicago's Trinity United Church of Christ. After a honeymoon on the West Coast, they moved into a condominium in the South Side neighborhood of Hyde Park.

New Jobs

Shortly after she and Barack wed, Michelle moved on to another new job. In 1993, she became the executive director of the Chicago chapter of a

Hyde Park

Unlike the majority of neighborhoods on Chicago's South Side, Hyde Park is a diverse community. About 41 percent of its residents are white, 39 percent are black, 12 percent are Asian, and 5 percent are Hispanic. The majority of the people in the community hold college degrees, and average incomes tend to be high. The neighborhood has more mansions than any other part of Chicago. Hyde Park is also one of the city's artistic and cultural centers with numerous museums, theaters, and restaurants. It is also home to the University of Chicago.

nonprofit organization called Public Allies. Barack had previously served on the organization's founding board and had suggested his wife for the position. In her new role, Michelle was responsible for getting the new chapter up and running. As with her earlier job change from Sidley to the mayor's office, this one involved a pay cut.

Public Allies was a program designed to prepare young people for leadership roles within their communities. The program trained the young people and set up internships for them with nonprofit organizations. The first thing Michelle had to do was find young adults to participate. In her recruitment efforts, Michelle met with college students and with young people living in public housing projects. Her goal was to bring together young leaders from all different backgrounds to help them

*Valerie Jarrett hired Michelle to work with her
as assistant to the mayor of Chicago.*

get used to working together. Participants in the
Public Allies program worked only four days a week.
Fridays were spent taking part in diversity workshops.

Some of the volunteers Michelle worked with best
remembered the way she challenged them to interact
with people who were different from themselves.
Beth Hester, a former Public Allies staff member,
said of her former boss, "Michelle reminded me
that it's too easy to go and sit with your own. She can

invite you, in kind of an aggressive way, to be all you can be."[2]

Michelle made the Chicago chapter of Public Allies into a success. She not only trained the young people who entered the program, but also raised money to fund its work. By the time she was ready to move on to another job in 1996, the organization had cash in reserve.

After working at Public Allies for three years, Michelle was hired by the University of Chicago as associate dean of student services in 1996. In her new position, she set up a community service program at the university, organizing student volunteers in a program similar to the one she had led at Public Allies.

A Political Spouse

The year before Michelle took the job with the University of Chicago, Barack had told her that he was

Encouraging Public Service

During her husband's 2008 campaign, Michelle reminded the young people with whom she spoke that she and her husband had left the corporate world to enter careers in public service. She called on today's generation of youth leaders to do the same and choose careers that would benefit their communities over those that would provide large salaries. Among the fields that Michelle encouraged young people to consider were teaching, nursing, and social work. Some people pointed out, however, that although the Obamas had left the corporate world, they had still benefited from it, including corporate donations to Barack's campaign.

interested in running for an open seat in the Illinois Senate. Michelle, who was skeptical of politics, was reluctant to give her blessing to this new venture. But she knew it was something her husband wanted to do, and she thought he would be good at it. She ultimately consented.

Once the decision was made, Michelle occasionally helped her husband campaign by attending fundraising events with him and charming his supporters. Barack won the election. In January 1997,

The Obamas' Marriage

During Barack's presidential campaign and the Obamas' first weeks in the White House, Barack and Michelle's marriage became a subject of interest to both the media and the public. Many people were enchanted by the couple's obvious love and respect for one another. Although the Obamas have acknowledged that their relationship has had rough patches, their friend Kirk Dillard said of their marriage,

Michelle and Barack have always been madly in love, they've always been best friends, and she's always been his closest confidante. Their relationship has remained constant at all levels, and it's wonderful to see.[3]

In a 1996 interview, Barack spoke of his attraction to his wife:

[S]he is at once completely familiar to me, so that I can be myself and she knows me very well and I trust her completely, but at the same time she is also a complete mystery to me in some ways. . . . It's that tension between familiarity and mystery that makes for something strong . . .[4]

Michelle has called Barack romantic, while he has said that she makes him laugh. She also is not afraid to tease him, even in public. On the presidential campaign trail, Michelle often talked about her husband's inability to put his socks in the hamper.

he was sworn in as an Illinois state senator. Michelle had no idea at the time the impact Barack's election would have on their family and their future.

Michelle and Barack were married on October 3, 1992.

Barack lost his 2000 run for the U.S. House of Representatives.

MALIA AND SASHA'S MOM

Michelle had long dreamed of having children. Shortly before Barack was sworn in as an Illinois state senator, she became pregnant with the couple's first child. Malia Ann Obama was born on July 4, 1998. At first, Barack shared childcare duties with his wife. The state senate was in recess, and he was on summer break from his teaching job with the University of Chicago. Michelle had three months off after her daughter's birth. She got up with the baby in the morning, while Barack stayed up with her at night.

This pleasant family situation lasted until the fall. Barack had to resume teaching and his recess in the legislature ended. Because the Illinois state capitol building is located in Springfield, Barack was often away from home for three days at a time. When he was in Chicago, he spent most of his time at meetings or attending to other work duties, such as grading papers. Michelle, too, returned to work, leaving her daughter with a babysitter while she was gone.

A Failed Campaign

The situation in the Obamas' marriage was already tense when Barack announced to Michelle

The Audacity of Hope

In Barack's book *The Audacity of Hope*, published in 2006, he wrote extensively about his and Michelle's marital struggles. He admitted to sometimes doubting his abilities as a husband and father. He acknowledged that most of the problems in their marriage were his fault and said that his girls were thriving mainly because of Michelle's skillful parenting.

After the book was released, Barack and Michelle appeared on the *Oprah Winfrey Show*. During the show, Michelle was asked if she still felt like she was raising her children alone. She admitted that she often did but said that she appreciated the way Barack focused on the family when he was home.

that he wanted to run for the U.S. House of Representatives in the 2000 election. She did not want him to do it. Barack later wrote,

> *When I launched my ill-fated congressional run, Michelle put up no pretense of being happy with the decision. My failure to clean up the kitchen suddenly became less endearing. Leaning down to kiss Michelle good-bye in the morning, all I would get was a peck on the cheek.*[1]

Even though his wife was barely speaking to him, Barack dedicated himself to campaigning. This meant that he was away from home more frequently. Unhappy with her husband's decision, Michelle still occasionally filled in for him at campaign events, but only if they fit easily into her schedule. She also defended Barack from critics who claimed that he was not "black enough."

Ultimately, the tension between Michelle and her husband helped Barack lose the election. The family was on their annual vacation in Hawaii in December 1999 when Barack received a call asking him to return to Illinois for an important gun control vote. Barack, however, knew that his wife was already angry. He had shortened their vacation in order to spend more time on the campaign trail. He did not want to make the situation worse. In addition, Malia had a bad cold. Barack did not want to leave Michelle to deal with their sick child alone. He stayed in Hawaii, and the bill was defeated by three votes. Both the governor and the media placed much of the blame for the bill's failure on Barack. Although he insisted that he had put his family's needs above his own career, Barack could not recover from the incident. He lost the election by a wide margin.

During his campaign, Barack had told Michelle that if his bid for Congress was

The Obama Daughters

As Malia and Sasha grew up, Michelle and Barack encouraged them to express their opinions and not to be afraid to ask questions. They also encouraged them to be mentally and physically active and limited the amount of television the girls could watch. By the time of the 2008 election, both Malia and Sasha played piano and tennis. Malia, who was ten, was also involved in dance, soccer, and theater. Seven-year-old Sasha participated in gymnastics and tap dancing.

Michelle and Barack established a number of family rules. The girls were not allowed to whine or argue, and they could not tease one another for the purpose of annoying. They also had to set their own alarm clocks and be in bed by 8:30 each night. If they did all their chores, including setting the table for dinner, making their beds, and keeping the closet in their play-room clean, the girls received an allowance of one dollar a week.

The family rules also included guidelines for birthdays. Michelle and Barack did not buy presents for their children, but they did spend hundreds of dollars on slumber parties. They said not buying presents was a way to teach their girls about limits.

unsuccessful, he would leave politics. Now that he had lost the election, she wanted him to do just that. When Barack was offered a job directing a foundation, Michelle encouraged him to take it. She said that the family needed the money. Both of them had student loans to pay off. Barack had maxed out his credit card to finance his campaign. Barack, though, was not yet willing to give up on politics.

INCREASING TENSION

Less than a year after Barack's unsuccessful bid for the U.S. House of Representatives, Michelle gave birth to the couple's second child. Natasha, usually called Sasha, was born on June 7, 2001. After Sasha's birth, Barack and Michelle's relationship deteriorated even further. Michelle had envisioned a life in which the entire family would sit down together for dinner every night. She was angry that her husband

Familial Stability

Michelle often made it clear that she considered her role as Malia and Sasha's mother to be the most important part of her life. When Barack decided to run for president, she was determined to keep her daughters' lives as stable as possible. As she hit the campaign trail for her husband, she enlisted the support of her mother, who left her job in order to help watch the girls. Although her mother was home with Malia and Sasha, Michelle still tried to limit her overnight trips to once a week so that she could connect with her daughters at the end of each day.

Michelle and Barack with their daughters Malia, left, and Sasha, in 2004

was gone so often, leaving her to raise their girls alone. She accused Barack of being selfish and said that she had not married him in order to become a single parent.

For his part, Barack could not understand why his wife was so angry. He thought he was giving as much of his time as he could to his family, along with all of his love, and that those contributions should be enough. He was hurt that when he was home he was given lists of chores rather than the affection he sought. Years later, Barack finally realized the strain Michelle had been under during this time:

> [N]o matter how much I told myself that Michelle and I were equal partners, and that her dreams and ambitions were as important as my own—the fact was that when children showed up, it was Michelle and not I who was expected to make the necessary adjustments. [2]

Taking Control

With the difficulties she was facing juggling work and caring for her children, Michelle considered becoming a stay-at-home mom. Instead, she decided to take control of her situation to make it more manageable. She realized that she had to accept Barack as he was.

Board Member

Throughout her career, Michelle has sat on the boards of numerous organizations. These include:
• Chicago Laboratory Schools, her children's private schools
• Otho S. A. Sprague Memorial Institute, a charitable organization funding research into the causes of disease
• Facing History and Ourselves, a nonprofit focusing on educating children about prejudice
• Muntu Dance Theatre, a South Side group performing traditional and modern African music and dance
• Chicago Council on Global Affairs, an organization that encourages discussion about global issues
• TreeHouse Foods, a corporate supplier to Wal-Mart (she resigned after her husband announced that he would not shop at Wal-Mart because of its anti-union stance)

Rather than trying to change him or becoming angry about the situation, she changed her own schedule. She found time for herself by leaving for the gym at 4:30 a.m. Barack got up with the girls to feed and dress them. She also hired a housekeeper to take care of the household tasks that she did not enjoy, such as laundry, cooking, and cleaning. And she asked her mother to help with childcare duties.

Not long after giving birth to Sasha, Michelle took another new job. She became the executive director for community affairs with the University of Chicago Hospitals. In this position, she worked to strengthen the relationship between the hospital and the surrounding South Side community, which did not trust the institution.

Michelle finally felt like she had found a balance in her life. She came to realize, as she later explained,

Bringing Along Baby

Michelle had a problem on the day of her interview with the University of Chicago Hospitals. She did not have a sitter for Sasha, who was still a baby. Rather than canceling the interview, she brought Sasha along. The baby slept through the interview, and Michelle was offered the job. Her boss later said that this incident was characteristic of Michelle: "It was, 'This is who I am, and this is my life.'"[3]

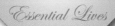

I cannot be crazy, because then I'm a crazy mother and I'm an angry wife. What I notice about men, all men, is that their order is me, my family, God is in there somewhere, but me is first. And for women, me is fourth, and that's not healthy.[4] ⌒

Michelle balanced her family with her career while Barack was frequently absent for political duties.

Michelle helped Barack campaign for the U.S. Senate election in 2004.

THE SENATOR'S WIFE

*J*ust as Michelle had finally gained stability in her life, Barack decided that he was ready for another attempt at a seat in Congress, this time in the Senate. Friends encouraged him to reconsider. They pointed out that a U.S. Senate campaign would put an even greater strain on his family than his unsuccessful House campaign had. While candidates for the U.S. House of Representatives campaign only within a specific congressional district, a Senate race is statewide. This meant that Barack would be away from home even more often than he had been during his last campaign.

Michelle, too, was against the idea of her husband running for another political office. This time, her concern was not only because she was skeptical of politics or because she did not want Barack to be away from home so often. She was also worried about money. Barack's credit card was maxed out. The couple also had a mortgage, student loans, and tuition to their children's school to pay for. Michelle worried that this new race might be a gamble that Barack would lose. And if he won, they would have to pay for two homes, one in Chicago and one in Washington DC. As she later explained,

> The big issue around the Senate for me was, how on Earth can we afford it? . . . My thing was, this is ridiculous, even if you do win, how are you going to afford this wonderful next step in your life?[1]

Road Trip

In the summer of 2004, the Obama family took an RV trip across southern Illinois. The trip was supposed to be a working vacation. The family could enjoy some quality time together while Barack also made campaign stops and introduced voters to his family. So many stops had been scheduled, however, that Barack and Michelle often spent the entire day campaigning. Campaign aids took the Obama children to amusement parks. In between stops, long hours were spent driving. The family covered 1,600 miles (2,575 km) in just five days. Afterward, Barack told his campaign staff to never put him or his family through a trip like that again.

Barack offered a solution to Michelle's concerns: he would write a book. Although he had already published his first book, *Dreams from My Father*, Michelle thought his idea was more of a fairy tale than a solution:

> And I'm thinking, "Snake eyes there, buddy. Just write a book, yeah, that's right. Yep, yep, yep. And you'll climb the beanstalk and come back down with the golden egg, Jack."[2]

Despite her continued reservations, Michelle was finally convinced by Barack's plea that he could help change the country if he were a U.S. senator. As he had in the past, he promised to leave politics if he lost the race. She joked that she hoped he would lose.

Barack's Campaign

In January 2003, Barack formally announced his candidacy for the U.S.

Senate. During the first stages of his campaign, Michelle was relatively uninvolved, although she did occasionally speak at campaign rallies. By summer 2004, though, she had become more active on the campaign trail and began to host fund-raisers on behalf of her husband.

In late July of that year, Michelle and Barack attended the Democratic National Convention in Boston, Massachusetts. Barack had been asked to deliver the keynote address. As Michelle waited backstage with her husband, Barack admitted that he was getting nervous. Wanting to break the tension, Michelle hugged him and said, "Just don't screw it up, buddy."[3] The two laughed, and Barack stepped onto the stage, where he delivered a speech that awed the 20,000 people in attendance, as well as the millions watching on televisions throughout the country. Suddenly, Barack and Michelle were famous.

Celebrities

After Barack's speech to the Democratic National Convention, Michelle had to get used to the idea that she and her husband were now celebrities. They were invited to events hosted and attended by other stars, such as the Legends Ball hosted by Oprah Winfrey. At these events, Michelle was surprised to find that stars including singer Queen Latifah were nervous about meeting her husband. She was also amazed that Barbara Walters felt the need to introduce herself; Michelle, like most people, already knew who the famous television journalist was.

After the convention, Michelle became even more involved in campaigning for her husband. She toured Illinois and gave speeches in which she talked about the problems that faced the middle class. She also became more personal, telling voters that she had fallen in love with Barack while listening to him speak in a church basement about how ordinary people could change the world.

The campaign was a success. On November 2, 2004, Barack was elected to the U.S. Senate. After the election, Malia asked her father if he was going to be president someday. The media picked up the question, and Barack denied that he had plans to run for the presidency anytime soon. Michelle believed him.

Staying in Chicago

In December 2004, Barack's plan to write a book to solve the family's financial problems panned out.

Still Putting Family First

After Barack became a U.S. senator in January 2005, Michelle did not treat him any differently than she had in the past. To her, he was still a husband and a father. This became clear to Barack during his second year in the Senate when he called home from Washington DC to tell his wife about an exciting development on a bill he had sponsored. She interrupted, telling him that there were ants in the house and that he needed to pick up some ant traps before coming home the next day.

The Obama family celebrates Barack's election to the U.S. Senate in 2004.

He was offered a nearly $2 million advance for a three-book contract. Suddenly, he and Michelle did not have to worry about money anymore, and they bought a mansion in Hyde Park.

Michelle and the girls would remain in their new home while Barack commuted between Chicago and an apartment in Washington DC. Although Barack had wanted to move the entire family with him to the nation's capital, Michelle wanted to stay near her work, her mother, and her children's school. She thought that Barack should be the one to make sacrifices for his political career.

Barack spent Tuesday through Thursday of each week in Washington DC. He flew home to Chicago for weekends. Although this meant that Michelle was again feeling the strain of single parenting, she did not feel the resentment toward her husband that she had in the past. She had figured out how to make their way of life work for her. She said that her children were

Adventure in Africa

During the summer of 2006, the Obamas traveled to Africa. They visited the countries of Ethiopia, Chad, Djibouti, South Africa, and Kenya, the home country of Barack's father. In addition to vacation activities, such as a safari in Kenya and a visit with Barack's grandmother, Michelle and Barack also confronted some of the serious issues that plagued these parts of the African continent. They visited the massive Kibera slum outside Nairobi, Kenya, where sewage and garbage filled open areas and residents lived in tin and canvas shacks. Barack and Michelle also volunteered to take HIV tests as a way of encouraging local people to get tested for the disease.

Wherever they went, huge crowds followed. People lined the streets to see Barack, chanting his name and jostling one another to get closer to him. Michelle was astounded by the attention her husband received. "It was completely overwhelming, it's hard to describe unless you were there," she said of their experience in one village. "To see hundreds and hundreds and thousands and thousands of people just lining the streets of this very small town, cheering this man, my husband."[4]

used to having a dad who was only around on weekends.

As she juggled her parental duties, Michelle also continued to work with the University of Chicago Hospitals. In March 2005, she was promoted to vice president for community and external affairs. She continued to help the hospital develop its relationship with the surrounding community. She increased the number of hospital staff who volunteered in the community while also bringing community members in to volunteer at the hospital. In addition, she set up a program to encourage local residents to seek early treatment at clinics rather than waiting until they needed the emergency room.

Even as Michelle tried to focus on her home and work life, questions continued to swirl around her husband's political future. Michelle focused on the present:

The Promotion

Michelle's promotion to vice president for community and external affairs at the University of Chicago Hospitals included a significant pay raise. In her former position, she made just under $122,000 a year; her new job paid nearly $317,000. Although some critics were suspicious of the fact that her promotion came just after her husband entered the Senate, the hospital's president insisted it was based on merit. He said that the hospital had offered Michelle the promotion previously but that she had turned it down because she did not feel she could handle the increased responsibility during Barack's Senate campaign.

I'm not wrapping my arms around more than what we are doing right now. You have to wait and see what happens, what the future holds and what makes sense. Timing is everything.[5] —

Michelle and Barack greeted the crowds at the
Democratic National Convention in 2004.

Michelle stood beside Barack in 2007 as he announced his candidacy for president.

FIRST LADY

When Barack was asked in 2006 whether he would run in the 2008 presidential election, he answered that it was up to his wife. He knew that if he ran without Michelle's support, his campaign would be doomed to failure.

For her part, Michelle was reluctant to approve of another disruptive political campaign. She knew how passionately her husband wanted this, though, and agreed to consider the possibility.

Before making a decision, Michelle met with Barack's advisers. She wanted to know how they would pay for the campaign, how much it would disrupt their family life, and how Barack would be kept safe. She also wanted to know what the campaign strategy would be and if Barack actually had a chance of winning. According to Barack's chief campaign strategist David Axelrod, "She was interested in whether it was a crazy, harebrained idea. Because she's not into crazy, harebrained ideas."[1] With her questions answered—and assured that Barack did have a realistic chance of winning the election—Michelle gave her approval.

No Smoking

Michelle's decision to approve Barack's run for president came with one condition: he had to quit smoking. She wanted him to be a good role model in the highly public role as a presidential contender. Michelle even announced her ultimatum on *60 Minutes*, calling on viewers to keep her husband accountable by calling her if they saw him with a cigarette. Although Barack admitted to still smoking occasionally on the campaign trail, he pledged not to do so in the White House.

The Closer

On a cold day in February 2007, Michelle walked with her husband and their children to the stage in front of the Old State Capitol in Springfield, Illinois. There, Barack announced his presidential candidacy. Then the couple got to work. Unlike Barack's previous campaigns, Michelle would play a significant role in his presidential bid. She scaled back her hours at the University of Chicago Hospitals so that she could spend time campaigning for her husband. She eventually took a leave of absence as the campaign intensified. Despite her commitment to the campaign, though, Michelle also remained devoted to her daughters. She pledged not to spend more than one night at a time away from home.

During the first few weeks of the campaign, Michelle's role was mainly to introduce her husband

"Our story is the great American story of success and pulling yourself up."[2]

—*Michelle Obama, Democratic National Convention, August 25, 2008*

at campaign stops. By March and April 2007, she was hosting her own campaign events. Even alone, she often drew crowds in the thousands.

In her campaign speeches, Michelle generally steered clear of talking about policy. She focused instead on her background on the South Side of Chicago. She stressed that she and Barack had lived through the same struggles as other men and women in the nation. She emphasized her concerns for issues that affected working women, military families, and those who had lost jobs.

Part of Michelle's role on the campaign trail was to show her husband's human side. She did so by poking gentle fun of him:

> *Don't get me wrong, I think my husband is a wonderful man with many skills and talents and he can take us to new places. He's a man who's just awesome, but he's still a man. . . . He still has*

Only Human

Michelle received some criticism for her tendency to talk about her husband's domestic flaws in her campaign speeches. She said her reason for doing so was to ensure that people did not have inflated expectations of her husband. "Barack is only human, and by mentioning some of his shortcomings I was hoping to make clear that he can make changes in this country, but it has to be with the help of everyone," she said. "The more we put people on those types of pedestals, the more we welcome disappointment."[3]

The Obama family appeared at the Democratic National Convention on August 28, 2008.

trouble putting the bread up and putting his socks actually in
the dirty clothes and he still doesn't do a better job than our
5-year-old daughter Sasha making his bed.[4]

On a more serious note, Michelle's speeches also addressed some voters' concerns that Barack was not experienced enough to lead the country:

> *Don't be fooled by people who claim that it is not his time. We are all too familiar with those baseless claims. . . . Don't be fooled by these claims because they are mere distractions. Distractions to keep us focused once again on what is not possible. . . . What we need right now is a leader. And a leader is more than a set of finite experiences.*[5]

In addition to her speeches, Michelle held a series of roundtable discussions with women around the country. She talked with them about the difficulties of being a working mother. She also met with military families to learn more about their struggles as their loved ones were deployed overseas.

Michelle enjoyed her role on the campaign—and she was good at it. She was given the nickname "the closer" for her ability to convince uncommitted primary voters to back her husband.

Michelle's part in the campaign was not without criticism, however. Some people felt that she was too negative. They did not agree when she called the United States a mean nation and focused on how hard life was for many people. They thought she should focus on the positive, including how she had risen from a working-class background to achieve great success. Michelle was especially criticized in February 2008 for saying,

> *For the first time in my adult lifetime, I am really proud of my country, and not just because Barack has done well, but because I think people are hungry for change.* [6]

Michelle later tried to clarify her statement, saying that she meant she was proud that voters were getting so involved in the election. However, many people took the remarks as unpatriotic and some began to characterize her as bitter.

A Softer Side

Michelle took heed of the criticism leveled at her. By the time Barack had secured the Democratic Party's nomination in June 2008 and begun his general election campaign against Republican candidate John

Rumors

During the course of the presidential campaign, a number of rumors surfaced about Barack and Michelle. In order to counter them, Barack's campaign established a "Fight the Smears" Web site. Among other items, the site dispelled rumors that Michelle had ordered a room service meal of lobster and caviar at a New York City hotel. She was not even in the city at the time. It also discredited a rumor that she had once made a video in which she used a racial slur. There was no such video.

McCain, she had softened her image. Her speeches were shortened, and their negative tone was replaced by a more optimistic note. She also began to do interviews with human-interest magazines, such as *People*, and made an appearance on the daytime talk show *The View*.

During the last few weeks of the campaign, Michelle crisscrossed the country, visiting key states in a final push before Election Day. She played an important role in the crucial state of Ohio ten days before the election, filling in for Barack after he left to visit his ill grandmother in Hawaii.

First Lady's Job

The role of the First Lady is not spelled out in the U.S. Constitution, and the position comes with no job description or salary. Because a First Lady has no official duties, each First Lady is free to define her own role.

The nation's early First Ladies primarily served as hostesses for White House receptions and dinners, and First Ladies continue to fulfill this role. By the early twentieth century, First Ladies had begun to combine the ceremonial role of hostess with more active political roles. In the 1930s and 1940s, Eleanor Roosevelt transformed the role of First Lady. She held her own press conferences and traveled the country on behalf of her husband. Many modern (and some earlier) First Ladies have also taken on their own projects. Lady Bird Johnson worked to promote the cause of environmental protection, and Nancy Reagan led an antidrug campaign. During the 1990s, Hillary Clinton took the role of the active First Lady even further by leading the development of a health care reform bill that ultimately failed.

In her first months in the White House, Michelle Obama began finding her own balance between raising her daughters and working on causes she felt passionate about.

Life in the White House

When ten-year-old Malia and seven-year-old Sasha moved into the White House, they became two of the youngest residents to live there since 1977, when Jimmy Carter's nine-year-old daughter Amy moved in. Despite their unique new home and all its amenities (including housekeeping services), Michelle was determined to keep life normal for her girls. She told the White House staff that she wanted Malia and Sasha to be able to continue to do their own chores, such as cleaning their bedrooms and making their beds, just as they had always done.

A New Life

In November 2008, the hard work on the campaign trail paid off. Barack Obama was elected the nation's next president. In January 2009, the Obamas began their new life as the First Family. They moved to Washington DC at the beginning of that month so Malia and Sasha could start the semester with their new classmates. The family lived in a hotel until the inauguration, after which they became residents of the White House. Michelle's mother moved into the White House to help raise her granddaughters.

As Michelle moved into her new home, she expressed a desire to see it filled with life and energy, and she made plans to redecorate the residence to create a family-friendly atmosphere. She also looked forward to eating dinners together as a family.

By spring, the First Family was settling into White House life.

Michelle held the Bible as Barack was sworn in as president on January 20, 2009.

Fulfilling a campaign promise Barack made to his daughters, the family welcomed their new dog Bo, a Portuguese water dog, on April 14.

Malia with the family's new puppy, Bo

DEFINING HER ROLE

Even before moving into the White House, Michelle made clear that her main role as First Lady would be as "mom-in-chief" to her two daughters.

At the same time, she intended to be involved in her husband's administration. Michelle's advice had long been sought by her husband, and he indicated during the campaign that he would continue to solicit her opinions once in office. In addition to the role of private adviser, Michelle planned to take on a more public role in addressing issues such as support for military families and working women who also had family responsibilities. She quickly planted a White House vegetable garden, the first such garden since World War II, hoping other families would follow her example. She also sought to encourage community service.

Within days of her husband's inauguration, Michelle took part in her first official act as First Lady. She hosted a reception for Lilly Ledbetter, the woman who inspired the first piece of legislation the president signed, the Lilly Ledbetter Fair Pay Restoration Act. She also visited several Washington DC schools and other institutions in an effort to get to know her new community. In February 2009, Michelle embarked on a tour of federal government agencies. These included the departments of Interior, Education, and Housing and Urban Development. She thanked employees for the work they had already done and encouraged them to get ready for the work ahead.

As the year progressed, it became rapidly clear that Michelle was becoming an international icon. Reporters followed her every move, as women everywhere tried to copy her fashion style. Soon, newspapers were comparing Michelle to such adored figures as Jackie Kennedy, wife of President John F. Kennedy, and Princess Diana of Great Britain.

In February 2008, nearly a year before taking on her new role as the first African-American First Lady, Michelle had talked about what the position would mean to her:

> *I think wow, what an opportunity. What a platform that I'll have, potentially, to talk about a whole range of issues that affect the country. What a privilege it will be to have the opportunity to speak to people's hearts, to be a part of moving this country in a different direction.*[7]

In 2009, that opportunity arrived.

*Michelle and Barack dance together on the night
of the presidential inauguration.*

TIMELINE

1964

Michelle LaVaughn
Robinson is born
on January 17
in Chicago.

1975

Michelle is accepted
to a gifted student
program at Bryn
Mawr Elementary
School in Chicago.

1981

Michelle graduates
from Whitney M.
Young Magnet High
School and enters
Princeton University.

1991

Michelle leaves
her job at Sidley to
take a new position
as assistant to the
mayor of Chicago.

1992

Michelle
becomes assistant
commissioner
of planning and
development for the
city of Chicago.

1992

On October 3,
Michelle and Barack
are married.

1985

Michelle graduates from Princeton with honors and enters Harvard Law School.

1988

After graduating from Harvard, Michelle takes a job with the Chicago law firm Sidley & Austin.

1989

Michelle is assigned to mentor Barack Obama, a summer associate at Sidley.

1993

Michelle takes a job as executive director of Public Allies Chicago.

1996

Michelle leaves Public Allies to become associate dean of student services at the University of Chicago.

1997

Barack is sworn in as an Illinois state senator in January.

TIMELINE

1998

On July 4, Michelle and Barack's first daughter, Malia, is born.

2000

Barack is defeated in a bid for the U.S. House of Representatives, and Michelle wants him to leave politics.

2001

The couple's second daughter, Natasha (called Sasha), is born on June 7.

2005

In March, Michelle is promoted to vice president for community and external affairs at the University of Chicago Hospitals.

2007

Michelle is present with Barack in Springfield, Illinois, as he announces his presidential candidacy on February 10.

2008

On February 22, Barack's campaign releases Michelle's Princeton thesis to the public.

2002

Michelle takes a position as executive director for community affairs at the University of Chicago Hospitals.

2004

On July 27, Barack speaks at the Democratic National Convention, propelling himself and Michelle to national fame.

2004

Barack is elected to the U.S. Senate on November 2.

2008

On August 25, Michelle gives a speech at the Democratic National Convention.

2008

Barack is elected president on November 4.

2009

On January 20, Michelle becomes First Lady as Barack is sworn in as president.

Essential Facts

Date of Birth
January 17, 1964

Place of Birth
Chicago, Illinois

Parents
Fraser and Marian Robinson

Education
- ❖ Whitney M. Young Magnet High School, Chicago, Illinois
- ❖ Princeton University, Princeton, New Jersey
- ❖ Harvard Law School, Cambridge, Massachusetts

Marriage
Barack Obama (October 3, 1992)

Children
Malia and Natasha (Sasha)

Residences
Chicago, Illinois; Princeton, New Jersey; Cambridge, Massachusetts; Washington DC

Career Highlights

❖ Attorney at Sidley & Austin, a corporate law firm in Chicago, 1988–1991

❖ Assistant to the mayor and assistant commissioner of planning and development for the city of Chicago, 1991–1993

❖ Executive director of the Chicago chapter of Public Allies, 1993–1996

❖ Associate dean of student services at the University of Chicago, 1996–2002

❖ Executive director and vice president for community affairs at the University of Chicago Hospitals, 2002–2009

❖ First Lady of the United States, 2009

Societal Contribution

Michelle left a career in corporate law to enter public service. She helped encourage economic growth in Chicago, trained young adults to become leaders, and helped increase volunteerism. After becoming First Lady in January 2009, Michelle planned to address issues facing U.S. families.

Conflicts

Michelle struggled with issues of race at Princeton. During Barack's presidential campaign, Michelle was accused of being unpatriotic. Michelle faced single-parenting challenges when Barack was away.

Quote

"Our story is the great American story of success and pulling yourself up."—*Michelle Obama*

ADDITIONAL RESOURCES

SELECT BIBLIOGRAPHY

Collins, Lauren. "The Other Obama." *New Yorker*. 10 Mar. 2008. 23 Jan. 2009 <http://www.newyorker.com/reporting/2008/03/10/080310fa_fact_collins>.

Lightfoot, Elizabeth. *Michelle Obama: First Lady of Hope*. Guilford, CT: Lyons Press, 2009.

Mendell, David. *Obama: From Promise to Power*. New York: Amistad, 2007.

Mundy, Liza. *Michelle: A Biography*. New York: Simon & Schuster, 2008.

Obama, Barack. *The Audacity of Hope*. New York: Crown Publishers, 2006.

Robinson, Michelle LaVaughn. "Princeton-Educated Blacks and the Black Community." 1985. *Politico*. 22 Feb. 2008. 24 Jan. 2009 <http://www.politico.com/news/stories/0208/8642.html>.

FURTHER READING

Brophy, David Bergen. *Michelle Obama: Meet the First Lady*. New York: Collins, 2009.

Colbert, David. *Michelle Obama: An American Story*. Boston, MA: Houghton Mifflin, 2009.

Young, Jeff. *Political Profiles: Michelle Obama*. Greensboro, NC: Morgan Reynolds, 2009.

Web Links

To learn more about Michelle Obama, visit ABDO Publishing Company online at **www.abdopublishing.com**. Web sites about Michelle Obama are featured on our Book Links page. These links are routinely monitored and updated to provide the most current information available.

Places to Visit

Chicago History Museum
1601 North Clark Street, Chicago, IL 60614
312-642-4600
chicagohistory.org/planavisit
The Chicago History Museum showcases the history of the city where Michelle Obama spent most of her life. The museum is open daily, and tickets can be purchased in advance. Audio tours are also available.

University of Chicago
5801 South Ellis Avenue, Chicago, IL 60637
773-702-1234
www.uchicago.edu
The University of Chicago is located in the Hyde Park community on the South Side of Chicago. Michelle worked at the school for several years, and it is only blocks from the Obama family's home.

The White House
1600 Pennsylvania Avenue Northwest, Washington, DC 20500
202-456-7041
www.whitehouse.gov/about/tours_and_events
In January 2009, the Obama family took up residence in the White House. The White House Visitor Center, which contains information about the mansion's furnishings and the families who have lived there, is open daily. Appointments are required for White House tours.

GLOSSARY

administration
　　Members of the executive branch of government, which is responsible for implementing laws, under a specific president.

affirmative action
　　A program that offers increased educational and employment opportunities for minorities and others who have been targets of past discrimination.

civil rights
　　Rights that all citizens of a country share, such as the right to vote; the civil rights movement focused on securing civil rights for African Americans.

community organizer
　　Someone who works to bring about social change by working with a community affected by a specific issue.

convention
　　A meeting of a political party to nominate a candidate to represent the party in an election.

diversity
　　Variety; a diverse community or group includes people of many different races, genders, or economic classes.

Great Migration
　　The voluntary movement of 7 million African Americans from the southern United States to the North between 1916 and 1970.

inauguration
　　A ceremony held for the swearing-in of a public official.

incumbent
　　The current holder of an elected office.

internship
　　A temporary job in which an employee, usually a student, gains practical, on-the-job experience in a specific field.

legislation
　　A law or laws.

minority
> Part of a small group within a society that differs from the rest of society in some way, often in terms of race.

multiple sclerosis
> A progressive disease that affects the nervous system, causing muscle weakness, tremors, partial or complete paralysis, and speech problems.

National Mall
> A national park that stretches from the U.S. Capitol to the Lincoln Memorial in Washington DC.

nominee
> A person selected for a specific position or office.

precinct captain
> A person who is responsible for organizing campaign activities for a political party in a specific part of a city.

primary
> Part of the election process in which a political party elects a candidate to run for a public office.

segregated
> Separated on the basis of race, ethnicity, gender, or other factors.

trademark
> A name or a symbol used to identify a specific product; a trademark is legally registered to the product's manufacturer so that no one else can use it.

transparent
> Open and accessible.

SOURCE NOTES

Chapter 1. Michelle Obama Speaks

1. "Michelle Obama Bio Video." *RealClearPolitics*. 25 Aug. 2008. Online video clip. 23 Jan. 2009 <http://www.realclearpolitics.com/video_log/2008/08/michelle_obama_bio_video.html>.

2. "Michelle Obama Democratic National Convention Speech." *Democratic National Convention*. 25 Aug. 2008. 23 Jan. 2009 <http://www.demconvention.com/michelle-obama>.

3. Ibid.

4. Ibid.

5. "Michelle Obama: A Challenge to Overcome." *BlackWomenForObama.org*. 25 Nov. 2007. 27 Jan. 2009 <http://blackwomenforobama.wordpress.com/2007/11/25/michelle-obama-a-challenge-to-overcome>.

6. André Leon Talley. "Leading Lady." *Vogue*. March 2009. 14 Feb. 2009 <http://www.style.com/vogue/feature/2009_March_Michelle_Obama>.

7. Mariana Cook. "A Couple in Chicago." *New Yorker*. 19 Jan. 2009. 27 Jan. 2009 <http://www.newyorker.com/reporting/2009/01/19/090119fa_fact_cook>.

8. Tonya Lewis Lee. "Your Next First Lady?" *Glamour*. 3 Sept. 2007. 26 Jan. 2009 <http://www.glamour.com/magazine/2007/09/michelle-obama>.

Chapter 2. South Side Girl

1. Jay Newton-Small. "Michelle Obama Finds Her Voice Too." *Time*. 24 Jan. 2008. 14 Feb. 2009 <http://www.time.com/time/politics/article/0,8599,1706706,00.html>.

2. David Mendell. *Obama: From Promise to Power*. New York: Amistad, 2007. 95.

3. M. Charles Bakst. "Brown Coach Robinson a Strong Voice for Brother-in-Law Obama." *The Providence Journal*. 20 May 2007. ProQuest. Web. 14 Feb. 2009.

4. Lauren Collins. "The Other Obama." *New Yorker*. 10 Mar. 2008. 23 Jan. 2009 <http://www.newyorker.com/reporting/2008/03/10/080310fa_fact_collins?currentPage=all>.

5. Liza Mundy. *Michelle: A Biography*. New York: Simon & Schuster, 2008. 51.

6. Lauren Collins. "The Other Obama." *New Yorker.* 10
Mar. 2008. 23 Jan. 2009 <http://www.newyorker.com/
reporting/2008/03/10/080310fa_fact_collins>.

Chapter 3. On to Princeton
1. Brian Feagans. "Georgian Recalls Rooming with Michelle Obama."
Atlanta Journal-Constitution. 13 Apr. 2008. 15 Feb. 2009 <http://www.ajc.
com/news/content/news/stories/2008/04/12/roommate_0413.html>.
2. Michelle LaVaughn Robinson. "Princeton-Educated Blacks and the
Black Community." 1985. *Politico.* 22 Feb. 2008. 23 Jan. 2009 <http://
www.politico.com/news/stories/0208/8642.html>.
3. Ibid.
4. Jay Newton-Small. "Michelle Obama Finds Her Voice Too." *Time.*
24 Jan. 2008. 14 Feb. 2009 <http://www.time.com/time/politics/
article/0,8599,1706706,00.html>.
5. Michelle LaVaughn Robinson. "Princeton-Educated Blacks and the
Black Community." 1985. *Politico.* 22 Feb. 2008. 23 Jan. 2009 <http://
www.politico.com/news/stories/0208/8642.html>.

Chapter 4. Studying the Law
1. Sally Jacobs. "Learning to Be Michelle Obama." *The Boston Globe.*
15 June 2008. 15 Feb. 2009 <http://www.boston.com/news/nation/
articles/2008/06/15/learning_to_be_michelle_obama>.
2. Charles J. Ogletree, Jr. "Reflections from an Obama Mentor."
Modesto Bee. 21 Jan. 2009. 26 Jan. 2009 <http://www.modbee.com/
opinion/community/story/571218.html>.
3. Richard Wolffe. "Barack's Rock." *Newsweek.* 25 Feb. 2008. 23 Jan.
2009 <http://www.newsweek.com/id/112849>.
4. Liza Mundy. *Michelle: A Biography.* New York: Simon & Schuster, 2008.
84.
5. Ibid. 85.

Chapter 5. Barack's Mentor
1. Liza Mundy. *Michelle: A Biography.* New York: Simon & Schuster, 2008.
92.
2. David Mendell. *Obama: From Promise to Power.* New York: Amistad, 2007.
93–94.

Source Notes Continued

3. Barack Obama. *The Audacity of Hope*. New York: Crown Publishers, 2006. 329.

4. "Barack Obama's Election Night Remarks." *Politico*. 4 Nov. 2008. 23 Jan. 2009 <http://www.politico.com/news/stories/1108/15294.html>.

5. Anne E. Kornblut. "Michelle Obama's Career Timeout." *Washington Post*. 11 May 2007. 29 Apr. 2009 <http://www.washingtonpost.com/wp-dyn/content/article/2007/05/10/AR2007051002573_pf.html>.

6. "Michelle Obama: The Full Interview." *CBS News*. 15 Feb. 2008. 15 Feb. 2009 <http://www.cbsnews.com/stories/2008/02/15/eveningnews/main3838884.shtml>.

7. Peter Slevin. "Her Heart's in the Race." *Washington Post*. 28 Nov. 2007. 15 Feb. 2009 <http://www.washingtonpost.com/wp-dyn/content/article/2007/11/27/AR2007112702670_pf.html>.

Chapter 6. Public Service

1. Scott Fornek. "Michelle Obama: 'He Swept Me off My Feet.'" *Chicago Sun-Times*. 3 Oct. 2007. 16 Feb. 2009 <http://www.suntimes.com/news/politics/obama/585261,CST-NWS-wedding03.article>.

2. Christi Parsons, Bruce Jaspen, and Bob Secter. "Barack's Rock." *Chicago Tribune*. 22 Apr. 2007. 23 Jan. 2009 <http://www.chicagotribune.com/news/nationworld/chi-0704220038apr22,0,3860794.story>.

3. "Obama Marriage Inspires Fascination, Imitation." *International Herald Tribune*. 12 Feb. 2009. 16 Feb. 2009 <http://www.iht.com/articles/ap/2009/02/12/america/Romance-in-the-White-House.php>.

4. Mariana Cook. "A Couple in Chicago." *New Yorker*. 19 Jan. 2009. 27 Jan. 2009 <http://www.newyorker.com/reporting/2009/01/19/090119fa_fact_cook>.

Chapter 7. Malia and Sasha's Mom

1. Barack Obama. *The Audacity of Hope*. New York: Crown Publishers, 2006. 340.

2. Ibid. 340–341.

3. Sandra Sobieraj Westfall. "Michelle Obama: 'This is Who I Am.'" *People*. 18 June 2007. 23 Jan. 2009 <http://www.people.com/people/archive/article/0,,20061177,00.html>.

4. Cassandra West. "Her Plan Went Awry, but Michelle Obama Doesn't Mind." *Chicago Tribune*. 1 Sept. 2004. 20 Feb. 2009 <http://www-news.uchicago.edu/citations/04/040831.michelle-obama.html>.

Chapter 8. The Senator's Wife

1. David Mendell. *Obama: From Promise to Power*. New York: Amistad, 2007. 151.
2. Ibid. 151–152.
3. Barack Obama. *The Audacity of Hope*. New York: Crown Publishers, 2006. 359.
4. Liza Mundy. *Michelle: A Biography*. New York: Simon & Schuster, 2008. 164.
5. Jeff Zeleny. "Q&A with Michelle Obama." *Chicago Tribune*. 24 Dec. 2005. 17 Feb. 2009 <http://www.chicagotribune.com/news/local/chi-051224obamamichelle,0,4172582.story>.

Chapter 9. First Lady

1. Gwen Ifill. "Beside Barack." *Essence*. Sept. 2007. 17 Feb. 2009 <http://www.essence.com/news_entertainment/news/articles/michelleobamabesidebarack?xid=121108-CNN-besidebaracklink>.
2. All Things Considered. "Michelle Obama: Family Is Focus Of Denver Speech." npr.org. 25 Aug. 2008. 29 Apr. 2009 <http://www.npr.org/templates/story/story.php?storyId=93944992>.
3. Allison Samuels. "Daring to Touch the Third Rail." *Newsweek*. 28 Jan. 2008. 23 Jan. 2009 <http://www.newsweek.com/id/96446/>.
4. Liza Mundy. *Michelle: A Biography*. New York: Simon & Schuster, 2008. 176.
5. Lynn Sweet. "Facing the Experience Question." *Chicago Sun-Times*. 15 Feb. 2007. 14 Feb. 2009 <http://www.suntimes.com/news/sweet/258066,CST-EDT-sweet15.article>.
6. Lauren Collins. "The Other Obama." *The New Yorker*. 10 Mar. 2008. 23 Jan. 2009 <http://www.newyorker.com/reporting/2008/03/10/080310fa_fact_collins>.
7. "Transcript: CNN Larry King Live Interview with Michelle Obama." *CNN.com*. 11 Feb. 2008. 17 Feb. 2009 <http://transcripts.cnn.com/TRANSCRIPTS/0802/11/lkl.01.html>.

INDEX

public service, 29, 32, 37,
39–40, 52–58, 68
speeches, 7–9, 13, 75–76,
84–89
thesis, 29–32
wedding, 54–55
Obama, Natasha (Sasha)
(daughter), 12, 65, 66, 69,
74, 86, 90
Ogletree, Charles J., 35–36

"Princeton-Educated Blacks
and the Black Community,"
29–32
Princeton University, 26–32
Public Allies, 56–58

Robinson, Craig (brother),
6–7, 17, 21–22, 24, 26–27,
29, 44
Robinson, Fraser, Jr.
(grandfather), 17–18
Robinson, Fraser, Sr. (great-
grandfather), 17
Robinson, Fraser III (father),
16, 18–22, 46, 49
Robinson, Jim (great-great-
grandfather), 17
Robinson, Marian (mother),
17, 18, 21–22, 69, 78, 90

Sidley & Austin, 42–46
South Side (Chicago), 8, 16,
19, 20–21, 47, 55, 56, 69, 85
state senate (Illinois), 58–60,
62–65

Torbert, Ronald, 40

University of Chicago, 19, 53,
56, 58, 63
University of Chicago
Hospitals, 69, 79, 84
U.S. House of Representatives,
63–65
U.S. Senate, 72–80

White, Quincy, 44
White House, 12–13, 54, 59,
83, 89, 90, 92–93
Whitney M. Young Magnet
High School, 23

ABOUT THE AUTHOR

Valerie Bodden is a freelance author and editor. She has written nearly 100 children's nonfiction books. Her books have received positive reviews from *School Library Journal*, *Booklist*, *ForeWord Magazine*, *Horn Book Guide*, *VOYA*, and *Library Media Connection*. Bodden lives in Wisconsin with her husband and their two children.

PHOTO CREDITS

Jeff Christensen/AP Images, cover; Ron Edmonds/AP Images, 6, 86; Charles Dharapak/AP Images, 10; Ted S. Warren/AP Images, 15; Polaris, 16, 33, 42, 71; M. Spencer Green/AP Images, 20, 77; Rick Bowmer/AP Images, 25; AP Images, 26; Jorge Salcedo/iStockphoto, 34; Obama Presidential Campaign/AP Images, 38; Steven Senne/AP Images, 41; Marc PoKempner, 48, 52; Saul Loeb/AFP/Getty Images, 51; Gerald Herbert/AP Images, 57; Obama for America/AP Images, 61; Frank Polich/AP Images, 62; Vandell Cobb/AP Images, 67; Scott Olson/Getty Images, 72; Charlie Neibergall/AP Images, 81, 95; Charles Rex Arbogast/AP Images, 82; Jason Reed/Reuters/Corbis, 91; Gerald Herbert/AP Images, 92